W9-DGF-430

BIOLOGICAL AND CHEMICAL WEAPONS

The Debate Over Modern Warfare

Biological and chemical weapons have changed the face of modern warfare.

BIOLOGICAL AND CHEMICAL WEAPONS

The Debate Over Modern Warfare

Allan B. Cobb

The Rosen Publishing Group, Inc.
New York

Published in 2000 by The Rosen Publishing Group, Inc.
29 East 21st Street, New York, NY 10010

Library of Congress Cataloging-in-Publication Data

Cobb, Allan B.
　　Biological and chemical weapons: the debate over modern warfare / Allan B. Cobb.
　　　　p. cm. — (Focus on science and society)
　　Includes bibliographical references and index.
　　Summary: Discusses the history and threats of biological and chemical weapons.
　　ISBN 0-8239-3214-1 (lib. bdg.)
　　1. Biological warfare—Juvenile literature. 2. Biological weapons—Juvenile
literature. 3. Chemical warfare—Juvenile literature. 4. Chemical agents
(Munitions)—Juvenile literature. [1. Biological warfare. 2. Chemical warfare.]
I. Title. II. Series.
　　UG447.8 .C63 2000
　　358'.38—dc21
                                                            00-008571

CONTENTS

As technology advances, the ability to make more powerful weapons increases.

INTRODUCTION

The year was 1915. World War I had been going on for more than a year. French and Algerian soldiers crouched in their trenches, waiting for orders to charge toward enemy lines and praying that the enemy would not launch an attack against them. Sometimes their charges against the enemy succeeded; other times they failed. Battle lines slowly moved forward and backward as each side gained and lost control. Between charges, troops spent long hours, even days, waiting.

All this would soon change.

At 5:00 P.M. on April 22, 1915, near Ypres, Belgium, modern warfare was revolutionized when German soldiers opened the valves of 5,730 cylinders containing chlorine gas. In all, they released 180,000 kg of chlorine gas. The greenish yellow clouds billowed toward the French and Algerian troops, burning their eyes and lungs

BIOLOGICAL AND CHEMICAL WEAPONS

Chemical weapons were first used in modern warfare near Ypres, Belgium, on April 22,1915.

Timeline

423 BC	1346	15th Century	1915	1925	1936
In one of the earliest recorded uses of chemical weapons, Spartans direct smoke toward Athenian forts, driving out the opposing army.	Tartar soldiers hurl plague-infected bodies over the walls of Kaffa, spreading bacteria to weaken enemy forces.	The Spanish conquistador Pizarro gives smallpox-infected clothes to South American natives, killing a large percentage of the South American population.	In the first use of chemical weapons on the modern battle-field, Germany releases 180,000 kg of chlorine gas against Allied troops.	The Geneva Protocol, which prohibits the first use of chemical weapons in warfare, is ratified by all major countries except Japan and the United States.	Tabun, the first nerve agent developed as a chemical weapon, is synthesized by German chemists.

and even killing some soldiers. In a panic, the French and Algerian troops fled their trenches, leaving an eight- or nine-kilometer-long gap in their line.

This was not the first time that a chemical had been used as a weapon, but it was the first time that such a chemical had been used on the modern battlefield. The results of this attack changed modern warfare forever.

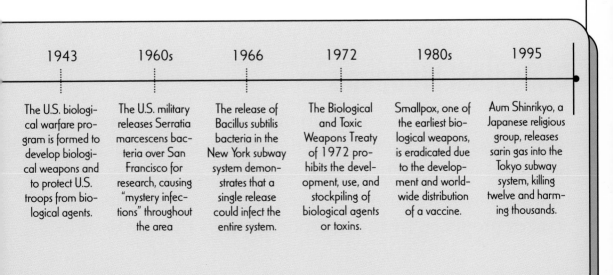

1943	1960s	1966	1972	1980s	1995
The U.S. biological warfare program is formed to develop biological weapons and to protect U.S. troops from biological agents.	The U.S. military releases Serratia marcescens bacteria over San Francisco for research, causing "mystery infections" throughout the area	The release of Bacillus subtilis bacteria in the New York subway system demonstrates that a single release could infect the entire system.	The Biological and Toxic Weapons Treaty of 1972 prohibits the development, use, and stockpiling of biological agents or toxins.	Smallpox, one of the earliest biological weapons, is eradicated due to the development and worldwide distribution of a vaccine.	Aum Shinrikyo, a Japanese religious group, releases sarin gas into the Tokyo subway system, killing twelve and harming thousands.

CHAPTER 1

WHAT ARE BIOLOGICAL AND CHEMICAL WEAPONS?

There is a long history of using biological and chemical weapons during times of war. These substances are intentionally used in battle as weapons of mass destruction, incapacitating, seriously injuring, and killing soldiers and civilians. Some biological and chemical weapons have ingredients that are active for short periods of time, whereas others can continue to remain active for a very long while.

Biological Weapons

Biological warfare is sometimes called germ warfare because germs, or bacteria, are the main ingredient of many biological weapons. Biological weapons are living, disease-causing microorganisms, or their toxins (poisonous substances produced by the microorganisms), that are used to harm or kill soldiers and civilians. In addition to bacteria and their toxins, viruses, as well as toxins produced by fungi, algae, and plants, are also used as biological weapons.

Whatever their source, biological weapons usually work by causing some kind of disease or illness that kills those exposed to it or makes them ill for a period of time. Some of the toxins used in warfare are far more deadly than any of the chemical weapons, which you will read more about in chapter 5.

Bubonic plague is one of the many biological weapons manufactured by scientists.

How Are Biological Weapons Released?

Biological weapons require some way of releasing the agent. One common method for dispersing biological weapons is in the form of an aerosol spray, which is a fine mist of liquid containing the biological agent. When the victim inhales the mist, the agent begins to take effect. Another way to spread biological agents is to add them to food, water, or other products that will be ingested by the intended victims.

Toxins

The toxins used as biological weapons are organic proteins that are naturally produced by organisms. The botulinum toxin, for example, which causes botulism poisoning, is one of the most toxic substances known today.

Research into using toxins as biological weapons began in the early twentieth century. At that time, it was difficult to produce sufficient quantities of toxins for use as weapons. Genetic engineering techniques developed in the late twentieth century, however, have made it possible to produce large quantities of these toxins.

One problem with using toxins as weapons is that they are usually sensitive to light or heat or are otherwise unstable outside of a laboratory. Advances in genetic engineering have made it possible to modify natural toxins to make them more stable. As a result, these genetically engineered toxins have become far more dangerous.

Genetic engineering has also been used to make the organisms of biological warfare stronger, more resistant to drugs, and easier to spread.

Chemical Weapons

What are chemical weapons, exactly? Technically, a soldier throwing sand (silicon dioxide) into the eyes of his enemy can be considered chemical warfare. A more realistic, useful definition of a chemical weapon is any substance, whether man-made or naturally occurring, that is used by the military to injure or kill humans.

Chemical weapons can be effectively delivered by artillery shells.

Chemical warfare agents enter the body through inhalation, absorption through the skin, or ingestion.

Chemical agents are classified into three main categories. Substances in the first category, such as tear gas, are known as harassing agents. Harassing agents are usually not lethal. They cause temporary irritation of the lungs, eyes, and skin.

13

Lethal agents are the second type of chemical weapon. As the name implies, these substances are usually lethal to their victims. Lethal agents are the type of agents that were used during World War I. Examples of lethal agents are cyanide gas, chlorine gas, and mustard gas.

Nerve agents are the third type of chemical weapon. These agents are usually classified as organophosphate compounds, which are organic compounds containing phosphorous. The most common use of organophosphates is as insecticides (chemicals used to kill insects).

As weapons, nerve agents are especially deadly because they inflict harm when absorbed through the skin or when inhaled. These agents are usually lethal even in very small doses. In addition, because the effects of nerve agents are not immediate, it is possible for many victims to be exposed to the substance before they are aware of the danger and can begin to take protective measures. Common nerve agents are sarin and VX.

Chemical agents are capable of killing thousands on the battlefield. One of the hazards of using chemical weapons, however, is the difficulty of protecting your own troops from the effects of the substance. Many chemical warfare agents stay active for days, sometimes even months, after their release. Factors such as a change in wind direction can determine who is affected by the agent and where the damage is done. During World War I, several incidences of surprise wind change caused chemical agents to affect the troops that had released the agent. Once it became possible to load chemical agents into artillery shells, the effectiveness of delivering chemical agents increased greatly.

Protection from Biological and Chemical Weapons

There are several ways to protect soldiers on the battlefield from biological and chemical weapons. Immunizations and vaccinations act to protect soldiers from some types of biological weapons. Soldiers can also be protected from direct exposure by using personal protective equipment (PPE).

MOPP gear protects soldiers from contamination.

BIOLOGICAL AND CHEMICAL WEAPONS

Personal protective equipment is any piece of equipment or clothing that shields or protects soldiers from physical, chemical, or biological hazards.

The gas mask is probably the best-known item of PPE. Gas masks filter hazardous chemicals out of the air before the wearer inhales. In addition, most gas masks cover the whole face, thereby protecting the eyes as well as the lungs. This is important because the eyes are particularly sensitive to many different chemical agents. PPE also includes various items that protect the skin, since some chemical agents can be absorbed directly through the skin.

The United States military has developed a PPE system called Mission Oriented Protective Posture (MOPP). MOPP is a flexible system that protects soldiers from contamination. MOPP is divided into five levels of protection, numbered 0 through 4. MOPP 0 is used in situations of minimal threat with no special gear required. MOPP 4 is used at the highest level of danger. At this level, soldiers are fully protected from breathing or touching any biological or chemical hazard. Having soldiers dressed in MOPP 4 gear severely reduces their effectiveness on the battlefield. The MOPP 4 gear is heavy, bulky, and very hot.

The Threat of Biological and Chemical Weapons

Almost all major nations in the world have signed treaties that prohibit them from being the first to use biological and chemical weapons on the battlefield. These international treaties do not prohibit countries from developing and stockpiling these weapons; all the treaties do is prohibit the first use.

The treaties state clearly that these types of weapons can be used in response to a biological or chemical threat made by another country. How are these treaties enforced? The hope is that if both sides are afraid of biological and chemical weapons—and both sides know that the other side has the same deadly weapons—neither side will use them. This threat is supposed to maintain a balance of power.

COMMON CHEMICAL WARFARE AGENTS

Lethal Agents
Chlorine gas
Cyanide gas
Phosgene gas
Nerve Agents
Sarin
Tabun
VX
Harassing Agents
Tear gas

Terrorism

All of the major nations of the world have stockpiles of chemical weapons, and some may have large amounts of biological weapons as well. The greatest fear is not that these weapons will be employed on the battlefield, but that they will be used by terrorists.

Many of the most deadly chemical agents are easily produced and many biological agents are easily cultured. The threat that terrorists will get ahold of these agents is extremely frightening because unlike soldiers on a battlefield, terrorists who use these substances in attacks are extremely difficult to single out for retaliation. A small terrorist group could kill thousands of people and no one would know for sure who was responsible.

In addition, the fact that there are so many chemical weapons used by different military forces around the world means that it could be easy for a terrorist group to steal what it needs. In fact, a few such attacks have already taken place, and the threat of more in the future is very real.

CHAPTER 2

THE HISTORY OF BIOLOGICAL WARFARE

One of the earliest known uses of biological weapons was in the sixth century B.C. Assyrians poisoned the wells of their enemies with wheat that was contaminated with ergot, a deadly fungus. Centuries later, the Romans threw dead animals into the water supplies of their enemies to infect the water with deadly bacteria.

Another early example of biological weapon use occurred in 1346, when the Tartars were attacking the city of Kaffa (known today as Fedossia, Ukraine). The city was surrounded by high walls, and the siege lasted for years. During that time, the Tartar army was struck by the plague. To weaken the city of Kaffa, the Tartars hurled the bodies of people who had died of the plague over the walls into the city, thereby spreading the bacteria to the enemy. The resulting epidemic in Kaffa caused the city to fall to the Tartars. Some historians think that some of the people infected with the plague who left Kaffa may have gone to Western Europe and spread the plague there. This may have been the beginning of the Black Death epidemic.

Smallpox was introduced to the New World by the conquistadors.

The use of biological warfare was not limited to the Old World, however. When the Americas were first discovered, biological weapons were used to weaken the Native American population. In the fifteenth century, the Spanish conquistador Pizarro is said to have given clothes contaminated with smallpox to the South American natives. Because smallpox was not found in the Americas, the natives had not built up a resistance to the disease. The resulting plagues killed a large percentage of the South American population. Similarly, during the French and Indian War (1754 to 1767), the English spread smallpox to the Native Americans who were loyal to the French by giving them blankets that came from smallpox hospitals.

Modern Biological Warfare

Biological warfare has become increasingly complicated, dangerous, and widespread in recent times. It is suspected that during World War I, German loyalists infected horses with glanders—a disease that weakens the horse and can be transmitted to humans—before they were shipped to France. In 1937, the Japanese began studying biological weapons and using aerosol sprays containing anthrax, a bacteria that causes flulike symptoms and can lead to death. They used anthrax as well as plague-carrying fleas in attacks on the Chinese.

Japan

By the time World War II started, Japan had stepped up its use of biological warfare against China. In 1941, Japan began spraying bubonic plague from planes over parts of China. In 1942, Japan developed special bombs to release bacterial agents. These bombs were soon determined to be ineffective and the program was stopped, but Japan's work in developing biological warfare agents prompted the United States to begin investigating the possibilities of biological weapons.

United States

The biological weapons program in the United States began in 1943 and continued until 1972. The United States government investigated many different biological agents, including those that cause diseases such as the plague, anthrax, botulism, tularemia, encephalitis, and brucellosis. The U.S. biological

The U.S. biological warfare program ran from 1943 until 1972.

warfare program had three major aims: to find biological agents for use in warfare, to protect troops from biological agents used by the enemy, and to determine the likelihood of an attack on the United States using biological weapons.

Great Britain

Great Britain began working with biological warfare during World War II out of fear that Japan and Germany would use biological weapons against British troops. Great Britain's research was centered around anthrax. The government set up a biological-weapons research lab on Gruinard Island, off the coast of Scotland. It chose that location because it thought the island was far enough from the mainland to protect people living on the mainland from contamination.

In 1943, however, there was an outbreak of anthrax along the coast of Scotland that faces Gruinard Island. As a result, the British government stopped all biological weapons testing and research on the island and attempted to decontaminate the island by starting a brushfire to kill the anthrax spores. Unfortunately, the effort was unsuccessful, and even today the island is contaminated with spores and off-limits to visitors.

Germany

Germany was not to be left behind in the race to develop biological weapons. The German government researched many different biological agents and ways to disperse them, but it did not actually use biological agents on the battlefield out of fear of severe retaliation by the Allied forces. More than anything else, Germany feared that the

United States had already developed the atomic bomb and would deploy it in response to Germany's use of biological weapons. As it turned out, however, Germany had overestimated the capability, and willingness, of the Allied forces to fight back.

How Effective Are Biological Attacks?

The United States military was, and still is, extremely concerned about the threat of biological weapons being used against the United States. In the 1960s, the U.S. military conducted tests to see how vulnerable large U.S. cities were to attack by biological weapons. One of the largest experiments involved a set of tests conducted many times over a number of years in the San Francisco area.

In these tests, the military sprayed a strain of bacteria called *Serratia marcescens* near the city. The bacterium is useful for this type of experiment because when grown a certain way, it turns red and therefore can easily be spotted in the air as it travels. The bacteria were released near the shore and were carried over the city by the sea breeze. The tests had an unexpected result, however: an increase in the number of "mystery infections" reported in the area. All of the patients with these mystery illnesses tested positive for *Serratia marcescens*. As a result, the military quietly stopped the tests.

Another experiment to test the susceptibility of the United States to biological weapons took place in New York

City in 1966. A bacteria called *Bacillus subtilis* was released in the New York City subway system. The results of the tests showed that the entire subway system could be infected from a single release. The winds created by the subway trains are sufficient to spread a biological agent quickly throughout the entire system.

The results of the San Francisco and New York City tests, as well as others, showed that the United States is quite vulnerable to biological attacks and that little can be done to prevent these attacks.

CHAPTER 3

THE HISTORY OF CHEMICAL WARFARE

There is a long history of the use of chemical weapons by military forces. One of the earliest recorded uses of chemical weapons was in 423 BC by the Spartans, who were attacking an Athenian fort during the Peloponnesian War. To drive the opposing army out into the open, the Spartans directed smoke into the fort. The thick smoke, which was from fires that were a mixture of coal, pitch, and sulfur, eventually drove the Athenians out of the fort. This action set the stage for using fire and smoke in warfare for many centuries to come.

In the seventh century AD, the Greeks developed a new strategy for using fire in naval warfare: a mixture called Greek Fire. No one knows the exact composition of Greek Fire, but it is believed to have been made of rosin, sulfur, pitch, naphtha, lime, and saltpeter. The mixture, which floated on water while burning, would float out to sea and eventually stick to the sides of enemy ships. Because all ships at that time were made of wood, they quickly burned.

In the fifteenth and sixteenth centuries, hollow explosive mortar shells were developed that could be launched over the walls of cities to spread various poisons to enemy camps. These shells were used to kill troops as well as to poison civilian food and water supplies.

Before the development of these mortar shells, chemical warfare was aimed at harassing enemy troops, making soldiers surrender or leave an area, or burning enemy ships in order to stop invasions. The development of mortar shells that could deliver poisons to an enemy forever changed the way that chemical weapons were used.

Modern Chemical Warfare

Modern chemical warfare began in the late eighteenth and early nineteenth centuries with the birth of modern inorganic chemistry. Interest in chemical weapons was renewed and intensified in the late nineteenth and early twentieth centuries due to the development of modern organic chemistry. Numerous plans to use chemical weapons against enemies were developed during the nineteenth century, but these plans were never used on a wide scale, since at that time, warfare was based on long-standing traditions and most officers felt that using chemical weapons was inhumane and against the rules of war.

BIOLOGICAL AND CHEMICAL WEAPONS

Some of the plans that were devised but never implemented were considered for use in many different wars by many different sides. For example, the British military considered and rejected a proposal to burn sulfur-laden ships before a beach assault against France in 1812. In another instance, in 1854, the British considered and later rejected the idea of using cyanide-filled shells to end a siege at Sebastopol during the Crimean War.

Similarly, the Union Army considered but ultimately rejected the idea of using chlorine-filled shells against Confederate troops during the Civil War. The French considered and rejected the idea of dipping bayonets in cyanide during the Franco-Prussian War. The use of poison chemicals was discussed at the Brussels Convention of 1874 and debated at the Hague Conventions of 1899 and 1907. None of these conventions was able to pass a resolution prohibiting the use of chemical weapons.

World War I

Chemicals were used for the first time on the modern battlefield during World War I. Germany introduced the newly devised flame thrower, though it met with little success due to design flaws. France used riot control chemicals similar to tear gas during several limited battles, but also met with little success. Then, on the afternoon of April 22, 1915, German troops released chlorine gas on the French and

Algerian troops near Ypres, Belgium. In all, about 800 soldiers died, and the rest of the troops quickly retreated.

Although this chemical attack did not kill a tremendous number of people, it was psychologically very damaging to the Allied forces.

To respond to German gas attacks, the British quickly began gathering cylinders of chlorine for use on the battlefield. British troops were issued gas masks that could protect

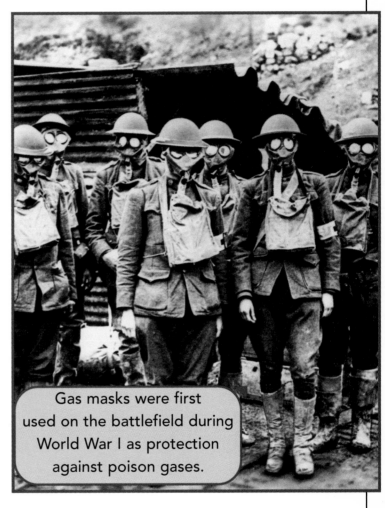

Gas masks were first used on the battlefield during World War I as protection against poison gases.

them against chlorine and cyanide gases. The British also introduced phosgene gas and several other poison gases. At the time, poison gases had limited potential use on the battlefield because each side knew that the other could respond to a gas attack with a gas attack of its own. As a result, as World War I continued, the use of chemical weapons became increasingly limited.

This all changed in 1917, however, when the Germans released a new chemical weapon. Again near Ypres, Belgium, the Germans sent artillery shells containing mustard gas into the Allied lines. Mustard gas was very different from the chemical agents that had been used earlier in the war. The gas had no strong smell, so troops did not know when they had been exposed; its full effects were felt after a few hours instead of right away; it stayed active for long periods of time; and it could be absorbed through the skin.

This first attack with mustard gas injured or harmed 20,000 victims. The sheer number of casualties overwhelmed the Allied medical system. The majority of the victims of mustard gas exposure did not die, but most of them required about six weeks to recover from the effects. Once again, the chemical attack by Germany delivered a psychological blow to the Allies.

Between the Wars

In the years between World War I and World War II, the international debate over the use of chemical weapons intensified. The 1925 Geneva Protocol prohibited the first use of chemical weapons in warfare. Chemical weapons could still be possessed by countries, but could only be used on the battlefield in response to a chemical attack by another country. The 1925 Geneva Protocol was ratified by all of the major powers except for the United States and Japan.

The 1925 Geneva Protocol prohibited the first use of chemical weapons.

In the late 1920s and early 1930s, the United States conducted little research into new chemical weapons; in contrast, Russia and Germany actively developed offensive and defensive chemical weapons systems. By the late 1930s, the German chemical-weapons program had developed nerve gas agents that were more deadly than any chemical weapon used in World War I.

BIOLOGICAL AND CHEMICAL WEAPONS

World War II

During World War II, all of the major powers had stockpiles of chemical weapons, but none of them broke the 1925 Geneva Protocol and used chemical weapons first. Germany had the most advanced and probably the largest stockpile of chemical weapons, but it overestimated the ability of the Allied forces to retaliate with chemical weapons. Fearing a massive retaliation, Germany never dared to use its chemical weapons on the battlefield.

After the War

In the 1950s and 1960s, all of the major powers, including the United States, continued to stockpile and research chemical weapons. The United States used herbicides to injure soldiers in parts of the jungle in Vietnam. The U.S. military also used irritants such as tear gas in both Vietnam and Laos. The United States only ceased to use chemical weapons in 1975, according to the terms of the Geneva Protocol, which was ratified in that year.

Many nations still have large stockpiles or the means of producing chemical weapons. For example, many of the countries that were once part of the Soviet Union still maintain stockpiles of chemical weapons. Similarly, many smaller nations such as Iran and Iraq are believed to have large stores of chemical weapons.

The United States has only recently begun to destroy its old and obsolete chemical weapons. It has set up a facility on Johnson Atoll, a small island in the South Pacific, to incinerate and burn these chemical weapons. Today, most of the chemical weapons that remain in the U.S. weapons arsenal are nerve agents such as sarin and VX.

Terrorists and Chemical Weapons

There are more than 50,000 different chemicals that could potentially be used as effective chemical weapons. These include common insecticides and herbicides as well as many other chemicals that cause blistering, choking, and poisoning. It is also possible to use psychoactive drugs such as LSD, commonly known as acid, as chemical weapons.

Chemical weapons can be used on many different targets. Terrorists can release chemical agents in crowded areas such as airports or subway systems, or contaminate food and water supplies or the ventilation systems of large buildings. All of these methods would succeed in creating mass terror. Because of the large variety of chemical agents available and the many different methods of releasing them, the threat of chemical weapons in the hands of terrorists is all too real.

CHAPTER 4

BIOLOGICAL WEAPONS

Biological weapons are used to kill soldiers or to make them so sick that they cannot fight. The most effective biological agents are the fast-acting ones. Almost any agent that causes an infection can be used as a biological weapon.

Common Biological Agents

Anthrax

Anthrax is a highly lethal infection caused by a naturally occurring bacterium called *Bacillus anthracis*. When used as a weapon, victims usually inhale or ingest the bacteria. Symptoms begin to show up between one to six days after anthrax enters the body. The initial symptoms of anthrax poisoning include fever, weakness, fatigue, cough, and mild chest pains. These symptoms are followed by severe respiratory distress and may lead to heart failure. Without treatment, death occurs in about 20 percent of victims. In some cases, death can occur only twenty-four to thirty-six hours after the onset of severe symptoms.

Anthrax cases are usually treated with high doses of antibiotics. Vaccines exist that provide a good measure of resistance to anthrax, but these vaccines are usually only available to military personnel and researchers. The vaccine must be taken in three doses at two-week intervals. Booster shots are needed every six months to a year to keep up the resistance. Protection from exposure to anthrax is usually achieved with personal protective equipment that filters the bacteria or spores from the air before the person breathes them in. Anthrax spores can remain active in soil for many years, making them a long-term problem in areas where they have been released.

Botulism

Botulism is a condition that results from poisoning by a toxin produced by the bacterium *Clostridium botulinum*. The bacterium is sometimes found in canned foods. If the cans are damaged or improperly made, the bacterium can begin to grow inside and produce botulinum toxin. If the food is then eaten, botulism results.

Botulinum toxin affects the central nervous system, causing paralysis of the heart and lungs. Symptoms of botulism include fatigue, weakness, dizziness, blurred or double vision, headache, nausea, vomiting, diarrhea, and abdominal pain. The fatality rate for botulism is 20 to 35 percent. Botulism can be treated with an antitoxin. There are seven different types of botulinum toxin, designated A, B, C, D, E, F, and G. Currently there are antitoxins for A, B, and E, and a vaccine is available for protection against types A through E. Most of the treatment for botulism is in the form of supportive care. The patient is closely monitored and placed on a ventilator if necessary.

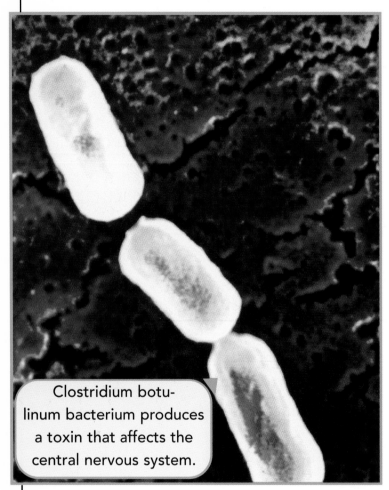

Clostridium botulinum bacterium produces a toxin that affects the central nervous system.

Botulinum toxin does not last long when exposed to the elements: After about ten minutes, the toxins react with other substances in the air and become harmless to humans.

Cholera

Cholera is an infection caused by a bacterium called *Vibrio cholerae.* The infection occurs when bacteria-contaminated food or water is ingested. Symptoms of cholera appear one to five days after exposure. Many infected people show no symptoms, but they act as carriers and can quickly spread the bacteria.

The symptoms of cholera include vomiting, abdominal pain, and excessive diarrhea, which causes severe fluid loss. The diarrhea can quickly lead to contaminated water supplies, and improper sanitation can also quickly affect food supplies. Patients with cholera can lose as much as 10 liters (2.5 gallons) of water per day. Without treatment, victims with symptoms will die rapidly.

With sufficient treatment, cholera patients recover quickly. They are treated with rehydrating fluids, intravenous fluids, and antibiotics. There is also a vaccine for cholera, but it must be administered several weeks before exposure, and a booster is required every six months. Unfortunately, the vaccine is only about 50 percent effective in preventing cholera.

The Plague

The plague is an infectious disease that is caused by the bacterium *Yersinia pestis*. The plague is usually transmitted by fleas, which bite infected people or rodents and then transfer the infection to other populations of rodents or humans as they move to a new host. The plague may also be spread through the air in aerosol form.

The plague occurs as two types—pneumonic and bubonic. The pneumonic plague primarily affects the lungs. The infection begins two to three days after exposure. The symptoms begin as high fever, chills, headache, and blood poisoning, then rapidly progress into labored breathing and lack of oxygen. Death eventually results from respiratory failure and circulatory collapse.

The bubonic plague begins two to ten days after exposure. The symptoms of bubonic plague include fever, weakness, and highly swollen, very painful lymph nodes, called buboes. The bubonic plague can then move into the central nervous system or the respiratory system.

Both forms of the plague are easily and reliably treated with antibiotics. Treatment is most effective if it is started within twenty-four hours of the appearance of the initial symptoms. There is also a vaccine available for the bubonic plague, which must be taken in several doses every six months for two years. Booster shots of the vaccine are required every year after the initial vaccination. The vaccine is not effective against the pneumonic plague. Exposure to the pneumonic plague requires doses of antibiotics for the duration of the exposure and for seven days afterward.

Ricin

Ricin is an extremely potent toxin that is extracted from the castor plant (*Ricinus communis*). Castor plants, which are used for making castor oil, can be found around the world. If ricin is ingested, it causes severe gastrointestinal distress, vascular collapse, and death. As a biological warfare agent, ricin is most often used in aerosol form.

Ricin, a deadly toxin, is extracted from the castor plant.

When inhaled, ricin acts as a cellular toxin. In the lungs, it destroys tissues and delicate blood vessels. Symptoms of ricin inhalation show up in about eight hours. These symptoms include fever, cough, nausea, tightness in the chest, profuse sweating, fluid in the lungs, and reduced blood pressure. The symptoms rapidly progress to respiratory failure and circulatory collapse. The amount of time between inhalation and death depends on the dose inhaled. In most cases, death occurs within thirty-six to seventy-two hours after exposure. There is currently no treatment or antidote available for ricin poisoning, although masks with filters that can remove aerosol particles can usually prevent exposure.

SEB

Staphylococcal enterotoxin B (SEB) is one of the toxins produced by the bacterium *Staphylococcus aureus*. The SEB toxin is a common cause of food poisoning. When ingested, the toxin causes nausea, vomiting, diarrhea, and intestinal cramps. Symptoms occur within a few hours of ingestion and continue for three to six hours. These cases are rarely fatal.

The toxin can also be used in biological warfare in aerosol form. After inhalation, symptoms appear in three to twelve hours. The symptoms are fever, chills, headache, cough, and chest pain. The fever may last from two to five days, and the cough may persist for up to four weeks. As with ingestion cases, inhalation cases are seldom fatal. There is no treatment for SEB poisoning: Today's antibiotics are of no use and there is no known vaccine.

Tularemia

Tularemia is a plaguelike infection caused by the bacterium *Francisella tularensis.* Typically, it is transmitted to humans through the bite of infected ticks or deerflies. It can also be spread through direct contact with infected rodents or rabbits, eating infected meat that is not adequately cooked, or drinking water contaminated with the bacterium.

The symptoms may appear one to ten days after exposure. Symptoms include headache, fever, chills, vomiting, and aching muscles. The lymph nodes of the elbows and armpits may also swell. This form of tularemia has a fatality rate of about 5 percent.

If used as a biological weapon, the bacteria would be released as an aerosol, leading to pneumonic tularemia (tularemia of the lungs). The pneumonic form would appear three to five days after exposure. The symptoms of this form are similar to those of the other forms, with the addition of a cough. The fatality rate would probably be much higher.

Tularemia can be treated with antibiotics; a vaccine exists to prevent infection, but it is only used on researchers who face a high risk of exposure.

CHAPTER 5

CHEMICAL WEAPONS

Chemical agents have many different names. Some of the agents are named for the chemical, others are named for their discoverers, and still others are given common names. To simplify and standardize the naming of chemical agents, they have been given two-letter designations. In the following descriptions, both the commonly used name and the two-letter designation are given for some of the more well known chemical agents.

Common Lethal Agents

Today, agents that are truly lethal—ones that are always lethal and for which no effective antidote exists—are seldom used because they pose a danger to soldiers on both sides.

CHEMICAL WEAPONS

Chlorine Gas

Chlorine (CL) gas was used in World War I. Since it is heavier than air, when released it would settle into the trenches used by soldiers. Chlorine gas is a greenish yellow gas that acts as an irritant to the eyes, nose, throat, and lungs. When it reaches the mucous membranes, it forms hydrochloric acid, which burns the tissues. As mentioned in the previous chapter, chlorine gas was the first lethal chemical agent used on the modern battlefield. It was quickly replaced with other agents, however, and is no longer considered a chemical weapon.

Phosgene

During World War I, chlorine gas was quickly replaced by phosgene. Phosgene (CX) is a colorless gas that has a smell similar to fresh-cut hay. The effects of phosgene gas are usually not felt for several hours after exposure. The symptoms of phosgene gas exposure are extreme coughing, frothing at the mouth, and asphyxiation (choking). During World War I, phosgene gas was responsible for about 80 percent of all deaths from lethal gases. Phosgene gas was stockpiled by many different military forces through World War II.

Mustard Gas

Another lethal gas used in World War I was mustard gas (HD). In its liquid form, mustard gas can range from colorless to amber-colored, and has a smell similar to burning garlic.

Mustard gas was first used as a weapon by the Germans against Allied troops on the night of July 12, 1917. The mustard liquid was loaded into artillery shells, which were then launched over enemy lines. When the shells exploded, the liquid vaporized (turned into a gas). Low concentrations of mustard gas can cause blindness, skin inflammation, redness, and blisters. High doses can lead to lung damage and asphyxiation.

Mustard gas was used as a weapon during World War I.

One year later, French and British troops began using mustard gas. All the major armies in the world continued to make and stockpile mustard liquid through the end of World War II.

Hydrogen Cyanide

Hydrogen cyanide (HCN) may or may not have been used on the battlefield during World Wars I and II, but it is suspected that Iraq used it against Iran in the 1980s. It was also used by Germany during World War II in gas chambers.

At room temperature, hydrogen cyanide is a colorless liquid with a boiling point of 26°C. The usual way it enters the body is through inhalation of the gas. However, hydrogen cyanide in the form of a gas, liquid, or solid can also be absorbed through the skin. Since the liquid is highly volatile (meaning that it changes quickly from a liquid to a gas), it has limited use on the battlefield because achieving a toxic level of cyanide before dispersal is very difficult. Hydrogen cyanide gas is much more effective in confined spaces.

The symptoms of cyanide poisoning depend on the level and method of exposure. When the poison is inhaled, the symptoms begin as restlessness and rapid breathing, accompanied by giddiness; headache; rapid, irregular heartbeat; and difficulty breathing. These symptoms are followed by vomiting, convulsions, unconsciousness, and respiratory failure. Exposure to a high level of gas results in sudden collapse and death.

There is no antidote for hydrogen cyanide poisoning. Exposure to a low level requires immediate medical attention; it is possible to reverse the effects of a low dose using chemicals to clean the hydrogen cyanide out of the blood.

Common Nerve Agents

Nerve agents, which are chemically related to many insecticides, are usually organophosphorus compounds—organic chemical compounds that contain phosphorus. The first nerve agents were developed in Germany during World War II. These generally cause intense sweating, filling of the bronchial (lung) tubes with mucus, dimming of vision, uncontrollable vomiting, convulsions, and finally paralysis and respiratory failure. Death from asphyxiation usually results within minutes when nerve agents are inhaled, or within hours if there is contact with the skin.

Tabun

Tabun (GA) was the first nerve agent developed as a chemical weapon. The scientific name of tabun is dimethylphosphoramidocyanidic acid. Tabun was synthesized by German chemists in 1936. Pure tabun is a colorless liquid with a fruity smell. If tabun is inhaled, the symptoms show up in about ten minutes. If tabun is absorbed through the skin, symptoms can take up to thirty minutes to show up. The symptoms of exposure to a low dose are constricted pupils, blurred and dimmed vision, chest tightness, and difficulty breathing. The symptoms of exposure to a high dose include drooling, sweating, nausea, vomiting, cramps, twitching, jerking, headache, confusion, drowsiness, convulsions, coma, and asphyxiation.

Sarin

Sarin (GB), another nerve agent developed by the Germans, was discovered in 1938. Sarin is a colorless and odorless liquid. It has been widely synthesized and stockpiled by military forces all over the world. The symptoms of exposure to sarin are roughly the same as those of tabun exposure. However, sarin is much more deadly because much less of it is needed to be lethal.

> **DID YOU KNOW?**
>
> Sarin vaporizes more than thirty times faster than tabun.
>
> Sarin is twenty-five times more deadly than cyanide gas.
>
> The lethal dose in humans is 0.01 mg per kilogram of body mass.
>
> Sarin was named for its discoverers: Schrader, Ambros, Rodriger, and van der Lin.

Sarin has a high density as a liquid. In gas form, it tends to drift above the ground for weeks or even months and can continue to affect military troops and civilians for long periods of time. Widespread use of sarin has never been documented on the battlefield, but it is suspected that sarin was used by the Iraqi military during an attack on the village of Birjinni in 1988.

VX

VX, another common nerve agent, was discovered in 1953. Like tabun and sarin, it is a colorless, odorless liquid. The effects of VX are similar to those of tabun and sarin, although VX is probably more dangerous than sarin because it is more persistent (remains present and potent for more time). VX can remain active as a gas for three to four weeks after release. VX is lethal in very low concentrations, making it very dangerous.

Other Nerve Agents

There are a number of other nerve agents, such as soman (GD), GE, CMPF, and VE. These have exposure times and symptoms similar to those of the other nerve agents. All of the nerve agents are particularly dangerous because they can be absorbed through the skin as well as inhaled. Protection against nerve agents involves using respiratory protection as well as complete covering of the skin with an impervious (nonpenetrable) material.

Harassing Agents

Harassing agents are chemicals that are not lethal but cause pain and injury. The most familiar of these is tear gas. Exposure to tear gas leads to watery eyes, coughing, and difficulty breathing. The symptoms of exposure begin immediately.

These agents are often used by law enforcement officers to drive criminals from confined areas or to immobilize rioters or dangerous individuals.

Harassing agents disperse rapidly and do not linger in the air. Harassing agents can also be found in small handheld dispensers designed for use against assailants. These personal defense sprays can also contain capsicum, the active chemical in hot peppers.

Tear gas is often used for riot control by law enforcement officers.

There are three types of tear gas, which are designated CN, CR, and CS. CS is the type most commonly used today.

The chemical name for CS is orto-chlorobenzylidene-malononitrile. At room temperature, tear gases are white

DID YOU KNOW?

VX tends to cling to everything it comes into contact with, making it the most dangerous of all the nerve agents.

Tabun is extremely dangerous—so dangerous, in fact, that a German workman died within two minutes after two liters of tabun were accidentally spilled down the neck of his rubber suit.

British casualties due to chemical agents during World War I are estimated at 185,000 injured and 8,700 dead.

solids. When heated, they decompose to make the thick gas that causes coughing and choking.

The effects of tear gas are most pronounced in humans. Dogs and horses are not very sensitive to tear gases. This allows police to use these animals in riot control situations when tear gas is used.

Tear gases cause almost instant pain in the eyes with excessive tearing and cramps in the eyelids. The gas also causes irritation of the mouth, nose, and throat. Exposure to a very high dose may cause vomiting. The irritating effects of tear gas persist as long as the irritant is in the air. The effects of tear gas disappear within fifteen to thirty minutes after exposure ends.

CHAPTER 6

THE THREAT OF BIOLOGICAL AND CHEMICAL WEAPONS

The Geneva Protocol of 1925 prohibits the first use of chemical weapons on the battlefield. Since all of the major countries of the world have chemical weapons in their arsenals that can be used to retaliate against any country that uses chemical weapons against them, some people feel that this is a strong enough deterrent to prevent the use of these deadly weapons. Others argue that a country that is all-but-defeated may choose to use chemical weapons as a last resort to inflict serious damage on its enemy. There is a growing movement to ban the production and stockpiling of chemical weapons in all militaries throughout the world.

But this is easier said than done. Chemical weapons are fairly easy to produce using industrial chemicals. It would be easy for one country to mass-produce chemical weapons without other countries detecting the production.

BIOLOGICAL AND CHEMICAL WEAPONS

The Geneva Protocol of 1925 also prohibits the first use of biological weapons or toxins. In addition, the Biological and Toxic Weapons Treaty of 1972 prohibits the development, use, or stockpiling of biological weapons or toxins. Thus officially, no country can possess any of these weapons. The true extent of the effectiveness of the Biological and Toxic Weapons Treaty is unknown, however. There are many rumors of countries conducting research into substances that could be used as biological weapons.

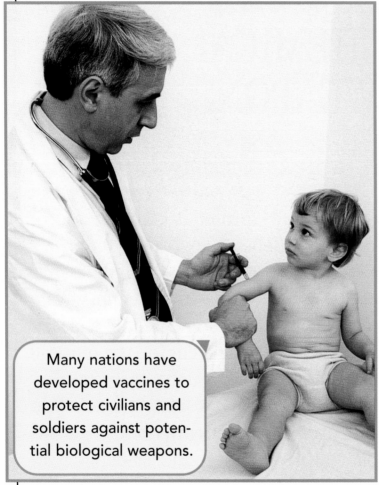

Many nations have developed vaccines to protect civilians and soldiers against potential biological weapons.

One complicating factor is that because of the large number of different potential disease-causing organisms that exist, determining what research is legitimate and what is illegal under the terms of the convention is extremely difficult.

For instance, one of the organisms used for early biological warfare was smallpox. Smallpox was used in the New World against the native populations of North America. As a result of research into smallpox, a vaccine was discovered to prevent it. The vaccine was made available worldwide, and smallpox was eradicated in the 1980s. Now many nations have programs to develop vaccines or immunizations for many of the other potential biological warfare organisms and toxins.

Terrorists and Biological Weapons

The greatest fear regarding biological and chemical weapons is the possibility that they will be used by terrorists. Biological weapons have all the characteristics that appeal to terrorist groups. First, these weapons are easy to conceal and difficult to detect. Normal procedures such as X-rays or trained dogs usually cannot detect them. Typically only a small volume is required, and it can be easily hidden. This means that chemical and biological weapons are easily smuggled into other countries.

Second, there is a time lag between exposure and symptoms. This gives the terrorists an opportunity to escape and lessens their chances of being affected—and caught. Third, biological weapons are very easy and cheap to produce and release. Fourth, they are equally effective whether they are used against a small target group or to infect large numbers of people in public spaces such as subways or airports. Finally, these weapons are directed at people and do not damage buildings or other structures. They do not involve the use of explosives of any kind. This makes biological weapons silent and deadly.

All of these factors come together to make a weapon that terrorists can easily use to strike terror into the hearts of their targets.

Terrorists and Chemical Weapons

Chemical agents are also attractive to terrorist groups, although these agents are more expensive to produce than biological agents. Furthermore, making chemical agents is somewhat more difficult than producing biological agents. Making chemical agents requires at least a modest laboratory, glassware, and certain chemicals. All of these are easily obtained, but they are much more expensive than what is needed for biological weapons. However, chemical agents have the advantage of lasting longer once they are released. Biological agents become inactive within a few hours of release, whereas some chemical nerve agents can remain active for days or weeks once released.

THE THREAT OF BIOLOGICAL AND CHEMICAL WEAPONS

Because it is easy to make a variety of chemical weapons and grow biological warfare agents, the potential for use by terrorists is high. In fact, there have already been several terrorist attacks using these chemical weapons. In 1995, members of the Aum Shinrikyo religious sect released sarin into the subway system in Tokyo, Japan. Thousands of people were injured, and twelve died as a result of exposure to sarin. The sarin was produced by the sect and was not very pure. Researchers who studied the

In 1995, the Aum Shinrikyo sect released deadly sarin gas into the Tokyo subway system, killing twelve civilians.

terrorist attack concluded that the poor quality of the sarin and inefficient dispersal methods kept the number of deaths relatively low. Had high-quality sarin and better dispersal methods been used, the attack could have killed thousands.

The threat of the use of biological agents such as anthrax prompted President Clinton to improve the U.S. Department of Defense's policy on antiterrorist chemical and biological weapons. Part of the program included immunizing all defense personnel against anthrax. In addition, about $1 billion was channeled into the development of antiterrorism programs.

Terrorist attacks aimed at crops could spread quickly and inflict serious damage.

Crops as Terrorist Targets

Terrorist attacks do not necessarily have to be launched against people. Using biological warfare, terrorists can attack food supplies and domesticated animals. Just like people, crop plants are susceptible to disease. Plant pathogens such as bacteria, viruses, and insects could easily be cultured in the laboratory. Using genetic engineering, crop pests could be engineered into "super pests" that are virtually unstoppable. Crops are an excellent target for this type of terrorist threat. Many plant diseases take a period of time to show signs in crops, allowing for large areas to be infected before anyone suspects that there is a problem. Also, because crops are grown in close proximity to each other, the plant disease can spread quickly. The same strategy can be used to kill domesticated animals such as cattle and sheep.

The Future of Biological and Chemical Warfare

As technology advances, the ability to make more powerful weapons increases. Genetic engineering has already enabled the production of large quantities of toxins and organisms with new and deadly properties. Chemistry has led to the manufacture of new chemical agents that are much more deadly than their predecessors. There is no reason to doubt that more chemical agents will be developed and made in the laboratory.

Although the goals of biological and chemical weapons research are often to develop weapons that are better able to kill, sometimes the research leads to positive advances. For example, as mentioned earlier, because of research into smallpox, a vaccine was discovered to eradicate it.

BIOLOGICAL AND CHEMICAL WEAPONS

There will always be a debate over the place of chemical and biological weapons. One side will argue that chemical weapons are needed to maintain a balance of power, whereas the other side will contend that just having these weapons creates the possibility of fatal mistakes. Some will argue that research into biological weapons will lead only to the development of new organisms that can be used destructively, and others will argue that the research can result in vaccines that protect everyone from these dangerous organisms.

Agreement over research into and possession of biological and chemical weapons is not likely to occur anytime soon. But the question of whether to stop it or to let it continue will surely be an extremely important issue in the future.

GLOSSARY

antibiotics   Medicine that restricts or stops the growth of microorganisms.

biological agent   Any disease-causing microorganism or virus used as a biological weapon.

Biological and Toxic Weapons Treaty of 1972   International treaty that prohibits research, use, and stockpiling of biological agents or toxins.

chemical agent   Any chemical used to incapacitate or kill.

Geneva Protocol of 1925   International treaty that prohibits the first use of chemical or biological weapons on the battlefield.

harassing agent   Any chemical (tear gas, for example) that is used to incapacitate but not kill.

immunization   Protection that allows a person to develop a resistance to a disease as a result of being injected with a live, modified form of a biological agent.

BIOLOGICAL AND CHEMICAL WEAPONS

lethal agents   Chemicals that kill those who are exposed to them.

MOPP (Mission Oriented Protective Posture)   Protocol set up by the U.S. military to dress soldiers in gear that protects them against a particular biological, chemical, or nuclear threat.

nerve agents   Chemicals that affect the nervous system.

organophosphate   A category of organic chemical compounds containing phosphorus that are used in many insecticides and nerve agents.

PPE (Personal Protective Equipment)   Protective gear worn to protect against a particular threat. PPE may include a respirator, goggles, gloves, and total skin protection.

toxin   A poisonous chemical produced by a biological organism that causes adverse effects in those who are exposed to it.

vaccine   Any preparation given to people to give them immunity to a particular biological agent.

FOR MORE
INFORMATION

Centers for Disease Control and Prevention
1600 Clifton Road
Atlanta, GA 30333
(800) 311-3435
Web site: http: //www.cdc.gov

Chemical and Biological Arms Control Institute
2111 Eisenhower Avenue
Alexandra, VA 22314
(703) 739-1538
Web site: http: //www.cbaci.org

Chemical and Biological Defense Information Analysis Center
Building E3330, Room 510
Aberdeen Proving Ground
Edgewood, MD 21010-5423
(410) 671-4878
Web site: http://www.cbiac.apgea.army.mil

FOR FURTHER READING

Ali, Javid, Leslie Rodrigues, and Jane's Information Group Staff. *U.S. Chemical-Biological Defense Guidebook.* United Kingdom: Jane's Information Group, 1997.

Cohen, Daniel. *The Manhattan Project.* New York: Twenty-First Century Books, Inc., 1999.

Hurley, Jennifer A. *Weapons of Mass Destruction: Opposing Viewpoints.* San Diego: Greenhaven Press, 1999.

McCuen, Gary E. *Biological Terrorism and Weapons of Mass Destruction.* Hudson, WI: GEM McCuen Publications, Inc., 1999.

Nishi, Dennis. *Weapons of War.* San Diego: Lucent Books, 2000.

Norris, John, and Will Fowler. *NBC: Nuclear, Biological, and Chemical Warfare on the Modern Battlefield.* Dulles, VA: Brassey's, Inc., 1997.

INDEX

BIOLOGICAL AND CHEMICAL WEAPONS

About the Author

Allan B. Cobb is a freelance science writer who lives in central Texas. He has written books, articles, radio scripts, and educational materials concerning different aspects of science. When not writing about science, he enjoys traveling, camping, hiking, and exploring caves.

Photo Credits

Cover © Superstock; p. 2 © FPG International Stock; p. 6 © Vincent Zuber/Custom Medical; p. 8 © Hulton Deutsch/Corbis; p. 11 © Ted Streshinsky/Corbis; p. 13 © Corbis; p. 15 ©Photri; p. 20 © Corbis; p. 22 © Peter Russell/The Military Picture Library/Corbis; p. 29 © Corbis; p. 31 © Bettman/Corbis; p. 36 © Superstock; p. 39 © Michael Boys/Corbis; p. 44 © Reuters Newsmedia/Corbis; p. 49 © Reuters News Media/Corbis; p. 52 © Mimi Cotter/ International Stock; p. 55 © Reuters/Kimimasa Mayama/Archive Photos; p. 56 © Uniphoto.

Series Design

Mike Caroleo

Layout

Law Alsobrook